BRITISH
KINGS &
QUEENS

First published in Great Britain by
CAXTON EDITIONS
an imprint of
The Caxton Book Company,
16 Connaught Street,
Marble Arch, London, W2 2AF.

ISBN 1 84067 061 4

1840 - 670 - 614 - 4413

A copy of the CIP data for this book is available from the British Library upon request.

With grateful thanks to Morse Modaberi who designed this book.

Created and produced for Caxton Editions by
FLAME TREE PUBLISHING,
a part of The Foundry Creative Media Company Ltd,
Crabtree Hall, Crabtree Lane,
Fulham, London, SW6 6TY.

Printed in Singapore by Star Standard Industries Pte. Ltd.

929.403

HEADstart

BRITISH KINGS & QUEENS

*Britain's rulers from
ancient tribes to today,
in glorious colour*

MAUREEN HILL

CAXTON EDITIONS

● Contents ●

Introduction

Two thousand years ago, when the Romans invaded and took control in England, Britain was divided into many different tribes, each led by a chief. These tribes and the areas they lived in developed into kingdoms and their chiefs became kings. The word 'king' comes from the Anglo-Saxon word 'cyning' which meant 'man of family'.

Kings were chosen from a royal family, but in the early years it was not automatic that a man's son would succeed him. A group of people came together to select the next king: in England the 'Witan', a sort of council, did this job. In later years it became accepted that the king's eldest son would automatically succeed him and if there were no sons, the nearest male relative. By the middle of the 16th century it was acceptable to have a female monarch if there were no sons to take the crown. Today the monarch's sons are still placed ahead of daughters in order of succession to the throne.

The role of the monarch has changed greatly over the last two thousand years – from being a leader in battle, through a period in which it was believed that they were directly chosen by God, to becoming something which is a symbol of the country. The monarch in Britain today has no power to make laws as they did in the past: over the years that power has been given to a Parliament elected by the people.

There are many rituals and splendid ceremonials associated with monarchy, such as the Coronation or the State Opening of Parliament, in which much of the history of royal Britain can be seen.

Roman Chieftains

Through archaeology we have learned about the way of life of the Celts, who lived in Britain before the coming of the Romans in 55 BC. The Celts had no form of writing and so it is from the writing of the Romans that we know of the details of their lives, such as who their leaders were.

Britain was divided into many tribes, like the Silures in South Wales and the Dumnonii in what is now Cornwall. These tribes had their own leaders, or kings, such as Cogidubnus, leader of the Atrebates in Southern England.

The most powerful leader in Britain before the Roman invasion was Cunobelinus, king of the Catuvellauni in Hertfordshire. His son Caratacus led the fight against the Romans. When Caratacus and his family were captured, they were taken to Rome and paraded through the streets – the Roman citizens were so impressed by his noble bearing that they secured a pardon for the family.

In about 60 AD, Queen Boudicca of the Iceni tribe led another revolt against the Romans. When Boudicca's husband, Prasutagus, had died the Romans had seized their land and treated Boudicca and her daughters cruelly. She led the Iceni, the Trinovantes and other tribes in the burning of Colchester, St Albans and London – killing thousands of Roman soldiers. Eventually Boudicca was defeated at a battle in the Midlands, after which she killed herself by taking poison.

Some of the Celtic tribes were allies of the Romans. For instance Queen Cartimandua of the Brigantes, a northern tribe, handed Caratacus over to the Romans when he tried to seek refuge with her.

Kingdoms of England

In 410 AD the Romans withdrew their troops and their citizens. Rome was under attack from tribes on the continent and everyone was needed to defend it. Soon after the Romans left people from north-west Europe invaded Britain. These were the Angles, the Saxons and the Jutes. England was once again divided into separate kingdoms which often fought one another for land and power. The most powerful king was given the title 'bretwalda'.

King Offa of Mercia reigned as bretwalda from 757 until his death in 796. Offa was a great king who came to control most of England and was respected throughout Europe. He organised a system of written laws and had silver coins minted with his portrait on them, but he is best remembered for the construction of Offa's Dyke: a huge barrier made of earth which runs along the Welsh border – it was constructed to keep the fierce Welsh tribes out of England.

Another important king from the period was Ethelbert, who was the first of the Saxon kings to convert to Christianity. In 597 Pope Gregory sent Augustine (later Saint Augustine) to convert the people of Britain to Christianity. King Ethelbert agreed to a meeting with Augustine but only if it was held out of doors as he feared what he thought to be the magic powers of the Christian monk. However, the following year Ethelbert was baptised as a Christian by Augustine.

In 1939 archaeologists discovered a buried Saxon ship at Sutton Hoo. Inside the ship was a wealth of Saxon treasure including musical instruments, weapons and armour, coins, jewellery and a magnificent iron helmet. It is thought that the ship burial was constructed for King Redwald of East Anglia who died in 627.

Alfred the Great

A new set of invaders came in 787, the Vikings whom the English called 'Danes'. For nearly 100 years the Scandinavians raided Britain for food, treasure and slaves. Then in 865, the Vikings decided to stay and overcame many of the Saxon kings.

In 871, the kingdom of Wessex was the only part of England not under Viking control. Its new king was Alfred, who had succeeded his brother Ethelred. Alfred fought the Vikings, saved Wessex and went on to reclaim much of England from the new rulers.

Alfred was an extremely wise king who well deserves his title 'the Great'. He ordered the building of 'burhs', a sort of fort where people could find protection if the Vikings attacked. He built a fleet of ships to help defend against sea attack and organised his fighting forces on a rota basis so that half the men would serve in the militia while the others tended their farms.

Alfred was not only wise when it came to fighting, he also brought in good laws and helped restore monasteries that the Vikings had destroyed. He knew that learning was important and valued the Anglo-

Saxon language. He learned to read when he was middle aged; translated four books from Latin into Anglo-Saxon and ordered the writing of many books in both languages.

Alfred died in 899 but by then the English were strong and his son Edward managed to gain control of the Viking lands, the 'Danelaw', making England one kingdom. Despite frequent Viking attacks the kings of Wessex were kings of a united England for all of the 11th century. Some of these kings, such as Athelstan and Edgar, ruled successfully but others, like Ethelred the 'Unready' (from the word *unraed* meaning evil-advice), did not.

The Coming of the Normans

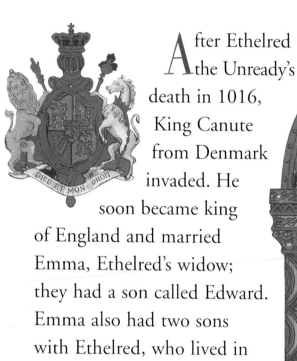

After Ethelred the Unready's death in 1016, King Canute from Denmark invaded. He soon became king of England and married Emma, Ethelred's widow; they had a son called Edward. Emma also had two sons with Ethelred, who lived in Normandy.

Canute ruled well but when he died in 1035 there were arguments over who would be king. Two of Canute's sons took the throne in turn until each died. Eventually Edward became king.

Edward was an extremely holy man, known as 'Edward the Confessor'. When he died in 1066 Harold of Wessex was pronounced King by the Witan. However, William of Normandy, a friend and distant relative of Edward's, claimed Edward promised him the English throne and prepared to attack. At the same time Harald Hadrada of Norway, a relative of Canute, was also preparing to invade and claim the crown.

Harold marched north to fight Harald Hadrada and defeated him at Stamford Bridge. He then learnt that William had landed near Hastings. The army rushed south but were too tired to fight well. Harold was killed and the English defeated.

William was crowned king on Christmas Day 1066 but the people did not welcome him and he had to find ways to control them. One way was to give the lands of the English nobles to his Norman followers who were given the title of 'baron'. He ordered a survey of everything in the country which was recorded in the *Domesday Book*; this allowed William to collect taxes accurately.

William was succeeded by two of his sons, William II and Henry I. Henry's only son drowned while crossing the English Channel. As a result, Henry's death started a civil war between his daughter Matilda and his nephew Stephen over who would rule.

The Magna Carta

Henry II was Matilda's son. His father was Geoffrey of Anjou, who had as his badge a sprig of the plant broom or *planta genista* in Latin – this is how the Plantagenets got their name.

Henry II is best remembered for being connected with the murder of Thomas à Becket, the Archbishop of Canterbury. Four knights murdered Thomas, who was later made a saint, in his own cathedral believing this to be the wishes of the king. Henry was shocked at the murder and lost some of the respect he had previously earned.

Queen Eleanor, Henry's wife, and their four sons often plotted against the king – despite this two of his sons died before Henry. In 1189, his son Richard succeeded him.

Richard was more interested in fighting in the Crusades than ruling England, earning the name 'Richard the Lionheart'. Richard spent only a total of five months in England during his ten-year reign and left the running of the country to his brother John who was hated by the people. This was partly because John constantly had to raise taxes to pay for Richard's Crusades and for Richard's ransom when he was captured.

When Richard died in 1199, John became king. He was a weak ruler and lost nearly all England's land in France. He was still disliked by the people and in 1215 the barons made King John sign a charter called *Magna Carta* to safeguard their rights. This changed the power of the king to govern the country as he liked. John's son, Henry III, later granted the barons the right to hold a Council and Henry's son, Edward I, gave the Council more power in return for money to pay for his wars. This Council was to develop into our Parliament.

The Plantagenets

Edward I was a good ruler in England but he was determined to make Britain a united country. He fought and defeated the Welsh princes and became ruler of Wales and then attempted to overcome Scotland – he tried many times, but failed. When he died in 1307 he was preparing to attack Scotland for a sixth time.

Edward II, son of Edward I, was a very weak king. He gave power and wealth to his friends and would not listen to advice. It is thought he was murdered.

In 1328 Edward III became king. He decided to reclaim the lands King John had lost in France. And so began the Hundred Years' War. In fact England and France were at war for 116 years. There was not continual fighting during this time, but a series of battles over the years. Apart for the war with France the worst thing that

happened during Edward III's reign was the plague – the Black Death. This affected the whole of Europe and between a third and a half of Britain's population died.

Edward III had a long reign and when he died in 1377 his son, Edward the Black Prince, was also dead. Although he was only 10 the Black Prince's son, Richard, was crowned.

As Richard II was only a child when he became king, his uncle, John of Gaunt (the Duke of Lancaster), ruled for him until he was old enough. Richard faced many problems. The first was a rebellion by the peasants who refused to pay taxes to pay for the wars with Scotland and France. Richard bravely faced the rebel leaders and ended the revolt.

Irish Kings

For many years Ireland had several separate kingdoms, such as Meath, Leinster and Munster, but from about the 4th century there was also a 'high king' (*Ard-Ri*), whom all the other kings recognised as their overlord. Cormac, the legendary first high king, established a ruling council at Tara. Others include Niall, the ancestor of the O'Neills who provided many future high kings. There was often fighting as to who would rule.

At the beginning of the 11th century Brian Boru fought to become high king. By this time the Vikings had begun to settle in Ireland and Boru was battling against both them and local kings. He was killed on Good Friday 1014, at the Battle of Clontarf – ironically his side had won and he was murdered by fleeing Vikings.

In 1166 the *Ard-Ri*, Rory O'Connor, banished the king of Leinster, Dermot McMurrough from Ireland. Some years earlier, Pope Aidan had given Henry II the right to be king of Ireland and when Dermot asked him for help Henry invaded. It was the beginning of the end for the kings of Ireland and the beginning of a long and troubled association between England and Ireland.

By the beginning of the 14th century the local Irish kings had lost their sovereignty. Their land had either been given to English noblemen or they had acknowledged the King of England as their overlord.

Over the years, resentment of the English overlords grew. In 1801 the parliament of Ireland was united with that at Westminster, but there were many calls for Ireland to become independent. When Southern Ireland eventually gained independence during the reign of George V it became a republic. Six counties in Northern Ireland remained as part of the United Kingdom, acknowledging the British monarch as theirs.

Lancaster and York

Richard II was a weak, quarrelsome king. When one of his advisors, John of Gaunt, died in 1399, Richard seized his land; this brought John's son, Henry Bolingbroke, back from exile. Many of the powerful nobles wanted Henry as king – Richard was captured and imprisoned in Pontefract Castle. He was never seen again and it is assumed he was murdered. Henry was crowned Henry IV.

In 1413 his son, Henry V, became king. He is regarded as one of the greatest of English kings, despite only ruling for nine years. He fought and won a famous battle against the French at Agincourt where his English soldiers were outnumbered four to one.

In 1422, Henry V's son, Henry VI, was crowned at only nine months old. By the 1450s a struggle for the crown had begun between Henry, a Lancastrian, and his cousin Richard, Duke of York. This became the Wars of the Roses. Each side had a different coloured rose as their badge: red for Lancaster or white for York.

There were many violent battles in this war and in one Richard of York was killed. However, his son, Edward IV, seized the throne in 1461. He ruled until 1483, with a brief period in 1470 during which Henry was restored to the throne.

When Edward died his twelve-year-old son Edward V reigned for three months. His uncle, Richard III, then took the throne and is assumed to have had Edward and his brother murdered after imprisoning them in the Tower of London.

Richard was disliked and distrusted. In 1485 he was killed at Bosworth Field in the final battle of the Wars of the Roses. Henry Tudor, a Welshman and Lancastrian supporter, was crowned king on the battlefield. He married Elizabeth of York, uniting Lancaster and York.

Welsh Rulers

For hundreds of years, like many other countries in Britain and Europe, Wales was divided into several separate kingdoms, each of which was ruled by a prince.

Until the coming of the Normans, most English kings were content to leave the Welsh alone or to have links with them as neighbours – Offa built his dyke to keep them out and Alfred had their support against the Vikings. The Normans, however, conquered southern Wales in the same way they had England. The kingdoms of North Wales fought fiercely and maintained their independence but they also fought amongst themselves over who would be the most powerful.

In Henry II's time one of the most powerful princes was Owain Gwynedd. He defeated the English in 1157 and 1165 with the aid of the long bow, a weapon, that had been developed in North Wales at this time.

By the 1230s Wales was under the control of one ruler, Llewelyn the Great, originally Prince of Gwynedd. In 1267 his grandson, Llewelyn II, claimed the title Prince of Wales. Henry III acknowledged this title as long as Llewelyn was prepared to pay homage to the English king. But when Edward I came to the throne Llewelyn II began raiding English border castles. Edward attacked, forcing the

Welsh to make peace in 1277, but five years later Llewelyn joined in a rebellion led by his brother Daffyd. Both brothers were killed and Edward assumed the rule of Wales, giving the title of Prince of Wales to his own son. Llewelyn was given the nickname 'Llewelyn the Last'.

The Tudors

Henry VII was a strong king who was careful with money – when he died in 1509 England was stable and relatively rich. His son, Henry VIII, liked spending money and living a luxurious life; he is best remembered for having six wives. His divorce from his first wife, Katherine of Aragon, caused Henry VIII to break away from the disapproving Roman Catholic Church and set up the Church of England.

The main reason for Henry marrying so often was his desire for a son – he believed that people would question the authority of a queen as ruler and that England would revert to a time when there was fighting about who should be monarch. His third wife, Jane Seymour, had a son, Edward. When Henry died in 1547, Edward was just nine years old and he died of tuberculosis when he was only fifteen.

Edward's half-sister, Katherine of Aragon's daughter Mary, became queen in 1553. At first she was popular but she earned the hatred of the people by trying to turn the country back to the Catholic faith. She was given the nickname 'Bloody Mary' because she had so many people executed for refusing to become Catholics. She even imprisoned her half-sister Elizabeth.

Mary had no children and when she died in 1558 the crown passed to Elizabeth – the daughter of Anne Boleyn and the third, and last, of Henry VIII's children.

Elizabeth was a popular and respected monarch, earning the nickname 'Good Queen Bess'. She was intelligent, well educated, liked to ride and hunt and to wear fashionable clothes. Elizabeth reigned well for 45 years. She never married and died in 1603 without having had any children.

Scottish Monarchs

For hundreds of years Scotland and England were enemies. Much of the animosity between the countries started with Edward I's attempts to take over in Scotland. Edward had been invited by the Scottish nobles to decide on who should be king when King Alexander III died. Alexander's granddaughter and sole heir, Margaret, died soon after. Edward decided on John Balliol, believing he could control him, but Balliol would not do as the English king wished so Edward invaded Scotland. He met with strong resistance from people like the legendary Scottish hero William Wallace.

English invasions continued in Scotland until the army of Edward II (son of Edward I), was defeated at the Battle of Bannockburn in 1314, by the new Scottish king, Robert the Bruce.

Up until the reign of Robert the Bruce, Scotland had not really been a united kingdom. Before 843, when Kenneth MacAlpin became king of a large part of Scotland, the land had been divided into four separate kingdoms. Robert helped to unify the country.

In 1329 Robert the Bruce died and his five-year-old son, David II, became king. David was a weak king who was captured and held to ransom by

Edward III; the cost of the ransom made Scotland a poor country. David also agreed that, when he died, Edward III's son would become king of Scotland which infuriated the Scottish nobles. However, when David died in 1371, Robert the Bruce's grandson, Robert Stewart (later Stuart) became king.

Three of the best known kings of Scotland are Duncan I, Macbeth and Malcolm III. These three kings feature in William Shakespeare's play *Macbeth* but Shakespeare's murderous version is not very accurate. Duncan *was* killed by Macbeth, but it was in battle. Macbeth also reigned well – he was Scotland's monarch from 1040 to 1057.

The Stuarts

When Elizabeth I of England died childless, the heir to the throne was James VI of Scotland; a member of the Stuart family. When he became King James I of England, he united the two thrones.

James was an unpopular king who spent money wildly, even though he did not have it. He forced banks to lend him money and increased taxes. He also angered Members of Parliament by insisting that he had a 'divine right', that is a right from God, to rule the country as he pleased. James was interested in all aspects of religion and he ordered a new translation of the Bible into English. It is the most widely read book in the English language.

James's son, Charles I, also believed in the 'divine right' of kings to rule the country as they pleased. During his reign he got into many arguments with Parliament over how the country should be run. These arguments developed into the Civil War. On one side were the Royalist supporters of Charles and the idea of a monarchy (they were known as 'Cavaliers'). On the other side were the 'Roundheads' who supported Parliament and the idea of a republic. Their leader, Oliver Cromwell, and his New Model Army finally beat the king's soldiers. Charles was captured, tried for treason and beheaded in 1649.

For 11 years Britain had no king or queen, instead it was a republic headed by Cromwell who died in 1659. In 1660 Charles II, who had fled to France, returned as king and was welcomed by the people.

When he died in 1685 Charles left no legitimate heir. He did have children but his wife, Queen Catherine, had none. The next in line to the throne was James, Charles's brother.

A Monarch
for Great Britain

James II was a Catholic and he tried to turn Britain back to being a Catholic country. This was very unpopular. The Duke of Monmouth, who was one of Charles II's illegitimate children, led a revolt against James soon after he became king. Monmouth's army was defeated, and he and 300 of his followers were executed.

In 1688 seven leading noblemen invited William of Orange, the Dutch king, to come to England to help get rid of James. William was married to James's daughter Mary who was a Protestant. When William and his army landed in Devon, he was welcomed by the people as he journeyed to London. James fled to France and William and Mary were crowned as joint rulers. This became known as the Glorious Revolution.

Mary died in 1694 and William died in 1702. They had no children and so Mary's sister Anne became queen.

During Anne's reign Britain became a powerful nation in Europe. Much of this was a result of defeating both France and Spain in war. Anne's reign is also associated with developments in science, literature and art, but one of the most important things to happen while Anne was queen was the Union of Scotland with England and Wales. From 1707 Anne ruled what was now called the United Kingdom of Great Britain.

Anne had 18 children, all of whom sadly died. After Anne's death her cousin, George of Hanover, became king. James II's son, James, had a closer claim to the throne, but he refused to stop being Catholic and, after the earlier religious troubles, a Catholic was no longer allowed to be monarch of Britain.

Hanoverians

George I was German; he was originally Elector (or king) of Hanover. Aged 54 when he became king of England in 1714, George never learned to speak English. He relied on Robert Walpole (regarded as the first British Prime Minister) to help him run the country. His son, George II, was born in Germany but did learn English.

In 1715 George I defeated a rebellion by Scottish clans loyal to the Stuart kings who, together with some English Tory nobles, supported the claim to the throne of the 'Old Pretender', James II's son, James. George II faced a similar threat from the Jacobites (from the Latin for James – *Jacobus*) in 1745. This time James's son, Bonnie Prince Charlie, led the rebellion. Although he had more success, like his father before him, the Prince was defeated.

George III was George II's grandson and he considered himself to be British rather than German. He was a gentle man, more interested in agriculture than government, earning the nickname 'Farmer George'. During his long and eventful reign, from 1760 until 1820, Britain fought the Napoleonic Wars; America declared and fought for independence; the Industrial Revolution took place; Britain gained more land with Captain Cook's exploration of Australia and the Pacific, and Ireland became part of the United Kingdom. Sadly, George III suffered periods of madness throughout his life and in 1811 was declared insane. His son took over as Prince Regent until his father's death in 1820, when he became king George IV.

George IV was succeeded by his brother, William IV, in 1830. During his seven-year reign William agreed to a major reform of Parliament, getting rid of MPs who had no constituency, and extending the vote to include some men from the middle classes.

Victoria and Edward

Queen Victoria was only 18 years old when she came to the throne. She reigned from 1837 until 1901, the longest reign of any British monarch. During that time Britain changed dramatically.

In Victoria's time as queen, Britain ruled a growing empire on which it was said 'the sun never set' – this meant that it covered so much of the world that it was always day somewhere under British rule. This empire made Britain an extremely rich and powerful nation.

For some Victorians life was extremely comfortable and, although there were still many poor people living in dreadful conditions, there were improvements in social conditions. Acts of Parliament prevented children from working in mines or more than 10 hours a day in factories. Schools were set up for some poor children. There was an increase in the number of men (though still not women) being allowed to vote in elections and Parliament became more responsible for the running of the country.

Victoria married Prince Albert of Saxe-Coburg in 1840. For 21 years they were extremely happy and produced nine children. When Albert died of typhoid in 1861 Victoria was devastated. She wore black mourning clothes until the end of her life and seldom went out in public following his death.

When her son, Albert Edward, came to the throne as Edward VII, there was more glamour and liveliness about the monarchy than in his mother's last years. However, there were growing problems. Poor people were beginning to complain about their living and working conditions and women were campaigning to be given the vote. There was also the prospect of war as the major countries in Europe, particularly Britain and Germany, tried to be the most powerful.

The House of Windsor

Edward VII reigned for only nine years; he was succeeded by his son George V in 1910.

In 1914 Britain went to war with Germany – this was the First World War. In 1917 George V changed the Royal family's surname of Saxe-Coburg to Windsor, in order to disclaim any association with Germany.

When George died in 1936 his son, Edward VIII, became king but he was never crowned. Like his father, Edward was popular and respected but in 1936 he asked to marry Mrs Wallis Simpson, a divorced woman. The government and church said that Mrs Simpson, although she could be the king's wife, could never be queen. Edward VIII would not accept this and chose to abdicate, that is step down as king.

Instead, Edward's brother, Albert, was crowned in 1937 as George VI. George VI was unprepared to be king; he was shy and had a stammer. Nevertheless, with the help of his queen, Elizabeth, George VI became a loved and respected king. During his reign Britain was once again involved in a terrible conflict with Germany – the Second World War. George VI died in 1952 and his daughter Elizabeth became queen.

Elizabeth has reigned over a Britain that has seen huge changes in society and technology and in the monarchy itself. Many of the people in the extended Royal Family no longer receive allowances from the state and the Queen now pays tax on her wealth. The divorces of three of her children and the death of Diana, Princess of Wales, mother of Prince William (the heir to the throne after his father Charles) have all been difficult for the Queen. Although there is respect for the Queen, people have begun to question the behaviour of her children and whether or not the monarchy will survive.

Further Information

Places to visit

British Museum, Great Russell Street, London, WC1B 3DG. Telephone: 0171 636 1555 – Sutton Hoo Treasures and much more.

Buckingham Palace, Victoria Street, London, SW1A 1AA. Telephone: 0171 930 4832 – present monarch's main residence.

Caernarfon Castle, Castle Ditch, Caernarfon, Gwynedd, LL55 2AY. Telephone: 01286 677617 – built during Edward I's reign.

Fishbourne Roman Palace, Salts Hill Road, Fishbourne, Chichester, PO19 3QR. Telephone: 01243 785859 – remains of the palace of Cogidubnus.

Hampton Court Palace, Surrey, KT8 9AU. Telephone: 0181 781 9500 – home of Cardinal Wolsey and later of Henry VIII. Has a famous maze and beautiful gardens.

The Palace Of Holyrood House, Edinburgh, EH8 8DX. Telephone: 0131 556 1096 – home to the Stuarts, including James I of England and VI of Scotland and Mary, Queen of Scots.

Houses of Parliament, Westminster, London, SW1A 0AA. Telephone: 0171 219 4272 – exhibits include portraits, paintings and Charles I's death warrant.

Kensington Palace, Kensington, London, W8 4PU. Telephone: 0171 937 9561 – birthplace of Queen Victoria and home to many members of Royalty; Princess Diana lived here.

Madame Tussauds, Marylebone Road, London, NW1 5LR. Telephone: 0171 487 0200 – waxworks of kings and queen.

National Portrait Gallery, 2 St Martins Place, London, WC2H 0HE. Telephone: 0171 306 0055 – portraits of many British monarchs.

Osborne House, York Avenue, East Cowes, Isle of Wight, PO32 6JY. Telephone: 01983 200022 – a favourite home of Queen Victoria.

HM Tower of London, Tower Hill, London, EC3N 4AB. Telephone: 0171 709 0765 – begun in the 11th century; has served as a royal home, a mint and as a prison.

Windsor Castle, Windsor, Berkshire, SL4 1NJ. Telephone: 01753 868286 – building first begun in 1078; restored after a fire in 1992.

Further Reading

Kings & Queens by Neil Grant, Harper Collins Gem
Tudors & Stuarts by Maureen Hill, Caxton Editions
Kings & Queens of England & Great Britain by
Eric R. Delderfield, David & Charles
The Kings & Queens of England by Nicholas Best, Weidenfeld & Nicholson
Towers in the Mist by Elizabeth Goudge

Web site

http://www.royal.gov.uk/index.htm – official Royal website with information about the Royal Family, monarchy through the ages and Royal Palaces.

Picture Credits

Mary Evans Picture Library pp. 8, 12, 15, 16, 18, 21, 22, 23, 26, 27, 32-33, 37, 41
The Bridgeman Art Library pp. 14, 17, 19, 20, 29, 36
Ivan J. Belcher pp. 24-25
Christies Images pp. 33, 34, 38, 39, 40
Visual Arts Library pp. 30, 31, 35